WORDS *of* HOPE *and* HEALING

THE
OTHER
LOSSES

Acknowledging *and* Mourning All Your Losses Along Life's Path

Alan D. Wolfelt, Ph.D.

Companion
PRESS

An imprint of the Center for Loss and Life Transition | Fort Collins, Colorado

Companion Press is an imprint of the Center for Loss and Life Transition, 3735 Broken Bow Road, Fort Collins, Colorado 80526.

28 27 26 25 24 23   6 5 4 3 2 1

ISBN: 978-1-61722-325-9

CONTENTS

WELCOME

If you're struggling with life's changes, challenges, and hurts, this book is for you.

Which means this book is for everyone, really.

Because every human life includes, among its many experiences, loss after loss.

From the time we're born, we learn what it feels like to be attached to something only to have it taken away. Babies love being swaddled and held. When they're put down and unwrapped, they cry. Why? Because they've temporarily lost their sense of being safe and loved.

As we get older, we gain, and we lose. We grow attached to family members, friends, neighbors, teachers, pets, homes, schools, activities, special belongings, and much more. Then when these relationships naturally change or come to an end, we feel a sense of loss.

In other words, we grieve—because that's what grief is: the difficult thoughts and feelings that naturally well up inside us during and after a loss.

Think back to your childhood. Which events or times were most difficult for you? When did you feel the most sad, hurt, or scared? Without doubt, these were loss experiences. Even when an anticipated loss did not come to pass, your fear that it might was still a loss experience.

Now, as an adult, you have probably experienced some significant losses. Some of them may have been the deaths of people you love. When we use the term "loss," this is most often what we mean. The death of someone in your life is, of course, a major loss. But so are many other relationship changes and transitions along life's path.

What's more, relationship changes are just one category of loss. We also feel loss when other things we value are harmed, changed, or placed at risk—things like health, careers, community groups, homes and other important belongings, even beliefs.

This little book is about all of these "other losses." Our culture doesn't always openly acknowledge them, but they can have a big impact on our lives, too. In fact, they can sometimes be as or more painful than death losses.

In the pages to come, first we'll talk about what the other losses are and why they bring grief into our lives.

Then we'll explore ways of acknowledging and mourning the other losses. This is essential because unacknowledged, unmourned losses too often result in prolonged pain. And if you're struggling with ongoing pain, mourning is how you will integrate your other losses and begin to heal.

Finally, we'll consider grief as a way of life. The ultimate goal is to learn to live each day acknowledging and celebrating or mourning whatever comes. Being present for all of it—the good, the neutral, and the bad—is the path to truly living and loving well.

Let's get started. I'm glad you're here.

PART ONE

LOSS AND GRIEF

"Grief is a reminder that love was present, and that even if it's no longer in its original form, that love still exists."

— Michelle Maros

WHAT IS LOSS?

Loss is when something you care about is threatened, harmed, or taken away from you.

Let's start with the "care about" part. If you were to make a list of all the people and things that matter to you in your life right now, you'd have a list of your current attachments.

Your list might look something like this:

My attachments

- Family members
- Friends
- Neighbors and colleagues
- Pets
- Work
- Health
- Home
- Community
- Favorite places
- Nature

- Faith and faith community
- Beliefs
- Groups
- Financial security
- Hobbies/interests

This is basically the list of the people and things you really and truly love or value. It's many of the elements that give your life meaning.

Some of your attachments are more central than others, of course. Your core attachments are those you feel you really couldn't (or wouldn't want to) live without. If I said to you— *Pick 25 people or things to keep in your life—everything else goes away*—who and what would you choose? Whatever makes the list for you are your core attachments.

LEVELS OF ATTACHMENT

CORE
—people, basic security
(health, home,
financial needs)

Outside your core attachments are other layers of people and things you care about. You might love your gym, for example, but is it a core attachment? It might or might not be. What about your job? What about the place you live? What about your passions for cooking or football? What about your TV? Where would you place each of them in the Levels of Attachment heart drawing?

The closer to the core an attachment is, the more difficult and painful the loss will be when it is threatened, harmed, or taken away in some way.

WHAT DO YOU MEAN BY "THREATENED, HARMED, OR TAKEN AWAY"?
Again, loss is when something you care about is threatened, harmed, or taken away from you. This can show up in lots of different ways.

A threat is a potential harm. If your marriage is rocky and there's talk of divorce, that's a threat. If you're considering moving away from a beloved home, that's also a threat. If you're awaiting a medical diagnosis and fear that it may be serious, you are experiencing a threat.

Possible dangers to your attachments are scary and painful no matter the outcome. And threats to things you care about are often an aspect of ambiguous or anticipatory loss as well (see p. 12).

THE OTHER LOSSES

Here's a list of common "other losses." It's not comprehensive by any means, but it will give an idea of the wide variety of common life experiences that are, in fact, losses.

RELATIONSHIP LOSSES

- Divorce
- Emotional separation
- Physical separation (inc. relocation, college, military service, incarceration, etc.)
- Estrangement
- End of friendships
- Volatile/hot-and-cold relationships

HEALTH LOSSES
(yourself or someone you care about)

- Injury
- Serious illness
- Chronic illness
- Terminal illness
- Infertility
- Dementia
- Loss of function (mobility, sexuality, eyesight, etc.)
- Aging-related diminishments

LIFE TRANSITIONS

- Infancy to childhood
- Childhood to adolescence
- Adolescence to adulthood
- Graduation
- Marriage
- Pregnancy
- Parenthood
- Relocation
- Empty nest
- Menopause
- Retirement
- Personal growth (emotional, spiritual, cognitive, career, financial, social, etc.)

COMMUNITY LOSSES

- Leaving or transitioning from a:
  School
  Neighborhood
  City
  Workplace
  Faith-based community
  Social group

WORK/CAREER LOSSES

- Transition from school to work
- Transition from one job or career to another
- Leaving workforce to parent or provide care full-time
- Layoffs or terminations
- Demotions
- Retirement

BELONGINGS LOSSES

- Financial
- Property
- Keepsakes and heirlooms

BELIEFS LOSSES

- Changes in beliefs about people you care about
- Religious or spiritual beliefs changes
- Political beliefs changes
- Social beliefs changes

MORE IDEAS

- What additional other losses spring to mind for you? Jot them down here.

_____

_____

_____

_____

WHAT ELSE WE LOSE

When we experience any of these other losses, in addition to losing the main object of our attachment, we may also lose other core feelings or values:

- Trust
- Security/stability
- Peace of mind
- Control
- Approval
- Belonging
- Personal history
- Sense of self
- Hopes and dreams
- And more

When someone or something you care about is harmed, on the other hand, they sustain a wound or damage of some kind. In the literal sense, when a loved one is injured in a car accident, that's a harm. In the rocky marriage I just mentioned, if one of the partners has an affair or treats the other partner badly, that's also a harm, even if divorce never occurs. If a friend develops a serious illness, that is also a harm. Why? Because not only is their life harmed, but their capacity to be present in your life may also be threatened or negatively affected. And if a home is damaged in a fire, that's a harm as well.

Finally, when something you care about is taken away from you, that means it comes to an end. Death is the ultimate example here, but other types of losses have their own finalities. Estrangement in a relationship can last forever. Graduation from a school and retirement from a job are typically everlasting changes. Divorce is the permanent dissolution of a marriage.

When you experience any of these types of losses, it hurts. The closer the attachment is to your core, often the more it hurts. And if it hurts, that's a sign you're grieving. The pain is a signal that your grief needs your attention and care.

WHY ARE THESE CONSIDERED "OTHER LOSSES"?

Obviously, we know that death is a significant loss. It's the one that often gets the most attention.

But as a culture, we're often not sure what to make of the other losses, or how to handle them. Actually, that's why we can label them as "other losses." If they're not death loss, they're an "other loss." And when our other losses aren't acknowledged and tended to—by ourselves and/or others—we can feel sad, confused, and hurt.

With death loss, we often have customs that let us know what to do. We rely on time-honored rituals to acknowledge the loss and express our grief and sympathy. We send and receive flowers. We share food. We get together and support one another through the use of ceremonies. The structure of these rituals helps hold us up at a time when we desperately need it.

However, we don't have such customs for acknowledging and supporting one another through the other losses. The social roles and rules are unclear. We may realize that the other losses can be quite painful, but we also tend to believe that they are not as worthy of grief, empathy, and public acknowledgment. This can create feelings of uncertainty, helplessness, and frustration.

What's more, the other losses often revolve around circumstances that are considered "private." If a couple separates, for instance, they may or may not make it generally known. Similarly, a cancer diagnosis may be kept quiet.

Infertility, too, may be a secret. And financial losses are usually confidential. Sadly, our unhelpful societal taboos and stigmas can keep us from openly sharing and supporting one another in our other losses.

It's my hope that together we can work on changing all of this. One reason I'm writing this book, in fact, is to wake us all up to the reality that the other losses are often significant as well. In general, we as a culture need better loss awareness. We also need better emotional intelligence, a skill that helps us communicate our own feelings and support others in theirs. And we need to work on breaking down more taboos and stigmas, because hiding the truth never helps anyone. The good news is that all of this can be taught, learned, and practiced.

WHAT ABOUT AMBIGUOUS, AMBIVALENT, AND ANTICIPATORY LOSSES?

Some of the most difficult other losses to acknowledge and cope with are ambiguous, ambivalent, and/or anticipatory.

Ambiguous losses are those that come with uncertainty or ambivalence.

Uncertain losses are situations that are typically in limbo or inhabit a gray area. Let's say you're experiencing physical symptoms suggestive of cancer and you're undergoing testing. During this time of uncertainty, you are naturally imagining a significant, if not life-threatening, harm to your health. This is a form of loss. If you have a good job that you love and you learn that your company may be downsizing in the coming year, something you care about is under threat. You may or may not lose your job, but the possibility, which you are forced to live with for some time, is also a kind of loss. Or imagine you are a parent whose teenager has begun acting out in risky ways. Again, this is a stressful situation no matter what, but part of the stress is projecting forward what the continuation or worsening of this behavior could bring.

Likewise, faltering friendships and family relationships can be ambiguous losses. Other examples can be meandering career paths and changes associated with aging. Uncertainty often causes apprehension, doubt, and anxiety.

Another type of ambiguous loss is one in which there is uncertainty about an attachment or relationship to begin with. If a work colleague leaves the company, for instance, you may find yourself feeling loss even though you weren't friends outside of work. Or if a wildfire burns a nearby community, you may experience grief without fully understanding why or feeling you have a right to.

Ambivalent losses are those for which you have conflicting feelings. For example, if you are trying to have a baby but have struggled with infertility for a year or two, you are no doubt distressed and dejected, but you may also at the same time be hopeful that any treatments you are pursuing will eventually work. You are living through a time of uncertainty and disappointment but also a period of expectation.

Divorce can also give rise to ambivalence—you may be happy to be finished with an unsatisfying relationship while also deeply hurt that your hopes and dreams did not come to pass.

Common life transitions can also cause ambivalent loss. For instance, when you graduate from college and take a job across the country from your hometown, you may be excited about your future and also sad that you're now living far away from your family. The same can be true of marriage, parenthood, and retirement. Happy changes are often simultaneously losses. I sometimes call these "sappy" losses. This is when you experience a combination of sadness and happiness at the same time. Every time you welcome something new, you give something up.

Anticipatory losses, on the other hand, are those that you can see coming in the future. You may naturally start grieving them long before they happen. When someone you love has dementia, for example, you begin experiencing smaller losses in the relationship right away. But you also may anticipate the coming larger losses associated with your loved one's memory issues. You know that one day your loved one may no longer be able to recognize you or feed themselves, and that the progressive disease will eventually take their life.

Not only are ambiguous, ambivalent, and anticipatory other losses confusing and anxiety-causing, but they often lead to what is called "disenfranchised grief." Remember how I said that the social rules and norms for the other losses are lacking? Well the social rules and norms for the more vague types of other losses are especially lacking. When your grief is disenfranchised, it means you're not considered someone who "should" be overly upset about whatever is happening. Not only is your grief not supported, but it may also be frowned upon. If, for instance, you just retired and have a great family who loves you, good health, and ample resources to live on, you shouldn't be sad, right?

However, the reality is that if you're experiencing a sense of loss about something, it is a loss. You have every right to grieve, mourn, and get the support you need and deserve.

LOSSES CAN BE BIG OR SMALL, MAJOR OR MINOR

Loss happens to all of us all the time, but not all losses are significant. If your favorite TV show gets canceled, for instance, that's a really trivial loss, right? But if a favorite person—your best friend, say—moves from across the street to across the globe, that's probably a major loss (even if the move is overall a positive change). And in between, there are lots of common life losses that we might consider medium-sized.

As I mentioned earlier, the more attached you are to someone or something, the greater your feeling of loss when there is a threat, harm, or ending. The same goes for the severity of the threat, harm, or ending.

The math of it looks something like this:

Strength of attachment **X** Severity & permanence of threat/harm **=** Degree of loss

So no, not every loss is major. But regardless of this equation, what I most want you to remember is that if a loss is bothering you, weighing on you, preoccupying your thoughts, regularly hurting your heart, impacting your daily life, or making you feel stuck, for you it's a significant other loss.

And no matter how minor a loss might look like to others from the outside, if to you on the inside it feels like a major loss, then it is. Always, you and you alone are the weigher and measurer of your own grief. I'm sometimes asked which grief is the worst. This reminds me that there is no competition between griefs. The worst is whichever you're feeling most deeply right now.

The Other Losses

ACKNOWLEDGING YOUR OTHER LOSSES

Maybe you picked up this book because you're struggling but you're not sure why.

One tricky thing about the other losses and grief is that you might not always recognize that some of the difficult thoughts and feelings you've been experiencing are really about the loss.

Let's say you've been irritable lately, and you think it's because your home life has been stressful. While it's possible that your home life is indeed contributing to your feelings of irritability and anxiety, with some introspection you might come to realize that your recent estrangement from your brother is mostly what's bothering you.

Or imagine that since the pandemic, you've found yourself less connected to a faith group that used to mean a lot to you. Maybe you're even feeling a sense of freedom and lightness about this change. Yet some days for no discernible reason, you're blue. You think it's because it's winter—cold and dark. But then you realize that some of your favorite faith community gatherings took place during winter. You may be experiencing ambivalent loss.

The other losses can sometimes be hard to discern and give attention to. As a result of our "grief-avoidant" culture, not everyone is skilled at recognizing the other losses and working to acknowledge and integrate them. Becoming more aware of your other losses and the impact they might be having on you can lead to insights that invite you to mourn them.

MY OTHER LOSS INVENTORY

One of the foundational principles of integrating grief into your life is that first, losses have to be acknowledged.

Now is a good time to make an inventory of all the other losses you are experiencing. Look over the list on pages 8 to 9 to spur your thoughts, then on the next two pages, make your own list. Which other losses are most bothering you, weighing on you, preoccupying your thoughts, regularly hurting your heart, impacting your daily life, or making you feel stuck?

Feel free to note past other losses as well as the more current ones. And if death loss is also contributing to your grief, include those losses, too.

When you have finished making your list, circle the other losses you think are most impacting you right now. These are the ones I suggest you focus on for the remainder of this book. Let's call them your Weightiest Other Losses, or WOLs.

The Other Losses

MY OTHER LOSS INVENTORY

_____

_____

_____

_____

_____

_____

_____

_____

_____

_____

_____

_____

_____

_____

_____

_____

_____

_____

_____

_____

_____

_____

PART TWO:
GRIEF AND MOURNING

"But there was no need to be ashamed of tears,
for tears bore witness that a man had the greatest
of courage: the courage to suffer."

— Viktor Frankl

WHAT IS GRIEF?

Now that you've given thought to what your WOLs may be, it's time to consider what you can do to integrate them into your ongoing life. This process starts with understanding what grief is.

Grief is what you think and feel inside of you about your WOLs. It's all your emotions. Grief often involves shock and numbness in the beginning followed by an ever-changing mixture of confusion, fear, sadness, anger, guilt, relief, and other feelings.

What feelings have you been having about your WOLs? Have your feelings changed over time? Do your emotions sometimes change day to day or even hour to hour? Here, jot down your most common or prominent grief feelings in recent days or weeks.

_____

_____

_____

_____

_____

_____

Grief isn't just feelings, however. It's also all your thoughts about your WOLs. Your brain likes to think about what it perceives as problems. It's built to try to figure things out, to understand what is happening and decide what to do about it. From an evolutionary standpoint, this tendency to think and imagine is what has enabled us as human beings to evolve and thrive for hundreds of thousands of years. In your own life, thought is what allows you to analyze, plan, and make decisions.

Loss is by its very nature challenging and complicated. It's an unwanted (or in the case of ambivalent loss, at least partially unwanted) change. So your brain sets to thinking about it. All your questions, imaginings, worry loops, what-ifs, worst-case scenarios, hopes, etc. about your WOLs—those are also a key part of your grief.

Below, jot down your most common or prominent grief
thoughts, questions, and worries in recent days or weeks.

_____

_____

_____

_____

_____

_____

Now that you've considered all your grief feelings and
thoughts, notice that they are invisible to others. They
take place inside of you, in your body and mind. You feel
your feelings in your body, and you think your thoughts in
your mind. The crucial act of expressing those feelings and
thoughts outside of you is what we'll talk about next.

WHAT IS MOURNING?

Mourning is the outward expression of your grief feelings and
thoughts. In other words, it's the behaviors of grief.

Crying is the classic example of mourning. It is instinctual to
cry when we're feeling grief because the tears of grief carry
stress chemicals out of the body. Have you ever noticed that
you tend to feel a sense of relief after a good cry? Tears also
alert others to the fact that we're upset and need empathetic

support. I believe that tears of grief are not only helpful, they are sacred.

Talking to other people about our WOLs is mourning, too.

First, when we put our grief feelings and thoughts into words, we are stepping through a learning process. The act of taking our often chaotic and shapeless feeling and thoughts of grief and making them more specific and concrete with language takes decision-making and effort. This is particularly true of talking about our other losses, because they are generally more nuanced, vague, hard to capture, multidimensional, and/or intertwined with other things. So, we learn about our grief from our other losses in part through this process of describing it.

And second, when we share those words with others, we're taking our inside grief and moving it to the outside. In this way, conversation is also a release and a means of getting the affirmation and support we need.

Besides crying and talking, other mourning behaviors include journaling, praying or meditating, hugging or holding others, looking over photos and mementos, taking part in loss rituals, making art or music, participating in a support group, and seeing a counselor. As you can see through these examples, there are many ways to mourn.

The magic of mourning is that it changes grief. It galvanizes it. It puts it into motion. It gives it momentum. And it often reveals it to others, inviting empathy, which in turn further enhances the healing momentum.

This process of converting grief into authentic mourning over and over again, day by day, week by week, softens the grief. It doesn't eliminate it, but it does make it more and more survivable, and less and less painful.

Think of grief as a wheel and mourning as the engine that turns the wheel. The wheel is absolutely necessary, but to get anywhere with it, you also need mourning.

Mourning is how you heal your WOLs. It's how you heal any grief, actually.

HEALING IN GRIEF

To heal the grief from your other losses is to become whole again. It's a holistic concept that embraces the physical, cognitive, emotional, social, and spiritual realms. You can never "cure" or "get over" your WOLs, but you can reconcile yourself to them. You can integrate them into your life so that you can live and love fully again.

When you have healed, your WOLs will no longer routinely bother you, weigh on you, preoccupy your thoughts, hurt your heart, impact your daily life, or make you feel stuck. Instead, they will be part of who you are.

MOURNING YOUR WOLS

To some extent, you may have already been mourning your WOLs. If you've shared any of your grief thoughts and feelings with people who care about you or cried about your losses, you have done some mourning.

But fully mourning grief—especially the ambiguous, disenfranchised, confusing grief of the other losses—requires a more active, intentional, in-depth approach. It takes time and attention. It is work with a purpose. The goal is a better life ahead. By allowing yourself to mourn well, you have the opportunity to go on to live well and love well.

There are six needs in mourning grief. Engaging with these needs is how you will more fully heal.

The Six Needs of Mourning

1. Acknowledge your losses

2. Embrace the pain of your losses

3. Explore memories of your attachments

4. Develop a new self-identity apart from the lost attachments

5. Search for meaning

6. Reach out to others for support—now and always

Let's take a look at each of the six needs and how you can meet them to integrate your WOLs into your ongoing life.

1. Acknowledge your losses

If you filled out the Loss Inventory on page 19, you've already begun working on this need. (If you haven't, I invite you to complete the inventory at this time). But fully acknowledging your WOLs will also mean being open about them with others.

Let's say you have a chronic illness and you naturally experience grief because of the limitations this illness has placed on your life. If you've been keeping a stiff upper lip about your illness around others yet at the same time grieving inside, you'll need to start being more honest about your natural and necessary grief with those who care about you.

Here's a good rule of thumb: If it's bothering you on the inside, that means you need to share it on the outside.

People are often afraid to be vulnerable. Grief can be seen as a weakness, especially when it comes to the other losses. You're sad because you moved from one nice community to another? You're feeling blue because you haven't spent as much time with a good friend lately? You may worry that these griefs will seem insignificant compared to the ostensibly bigger, more pressing concerns of others.

But again, the only true measure of a loss is how it makes you feel and think inside. If any losses feel weighty to you, then they're significant. And owning them means learning to feel justified and secure in talking about them with others.

So I urge you to build relationships that allow for honesty and vulnerability. Think about your friends and family members. Who among them are the best, most nonjudgmental listeners? These are your people when it comes to acknowledging your WOLs.

If you know someone who has experienced a similar loss, this can be a great point of connection. If you're struggling with the losses of parenthood, for example—balancing family with individuality—then seek out other parents to talk to about this loss.

2. *Embrace the pain of your losses*

Embracing the pain of your WOLs means a few things.

First it means acknowledging the appropriateness of the pain. You are attached to someone or something, and now that relationship, person, or thing has been threatened, harmed, or ended. Of course it hurts! Of course the pain makes sense!

Second, embracing the pain means understanding that it is there for a reason. Like physical pain after an injury, the emotional and spiritual pain of grief draws our attention to our grief wound and forces us to pay attention to it. The pain causes us to turn inward and do the work of the other five needs of mourning, which are necessary for our eventual integration of life losses. We need the pain or we could be stuck forever.

And third, embracing the pain means learning to regard the pain as part of our love. Without love, there is no emotional pain in life. If we accept that love is a gift—the best we human beings get to experience, in fact—then we must also come to accept that grief, which is part and parcel of love, is a sort of gift as well.

In other words, if your love is good and valuable, then so, too, is your grief. You may have heard it said that you need to feel it to heal it. While this may sound simple, it's a profound truth when it comes to integrating losses into our lives.

So those are the theoretical justifications for embracing the pain of grief. On a practical level, embracing the pain of your losses involves expressing it in various ways.

Telling others about why you're hurting and how you feel is the core of this need of mourning. If you've got good, empathetic friends and close family members you can talk to, start there.

Support groups pertaining to your WOLs can be a potential option to outwardly embrace your pain. If you're divorcing, for example, you might find a divorce support group extremely helpful. For some people, online groups can be another potential source of support. In an appropriate support group that matches your needs, you're likely to meet others who share your experience and have many feelings and thoughts in common. I often find there's no substitute for being with others who share similar losses.

Talking to a grief counselor is also a potential way to help meet this mourning need. Grief counselors are trained to understand that grief is the natural result of many types of losses, not just death. A compassionate and grief-informed counselor can also help you tease apart your grief from multiple losses. It could be that your WOLs have created a complex blend of grief that may require some thought and discussion to understand and fully mourn.

What's more, a grief counselor can help you understand and embrace your pain in cases of complicated grief. Complicated grief is grief that stems from complicated loss experiences. If any of your WOLs or death losses were traumatic or associated with violence, abuse, betrayal, multiple losses in one incident or close together in time, or any circumstances that seem especially challenging, seeing a grief counselor is a good idea. The other losses can get really complicated, especially when they are traumatic or stack up over time. Slowly and carefully unpacking everything that happened in the safety of a counselor's office may well be just the support you need to work on all six of the needs of mourning and step toward healing.

Other ways of embracing and expressing pain include making art, dancing or other intentional physical movement, writing stories or poetry, praying or meditating on your pain, and taking part in grief rituals.

DOSING YOUR GRIEF

As you work on actively, authentically mourning your WOLs with the six needs, you'll find that it isn't possible to be mourning all the time. Grief work is often exhausting—physically, emotionally, and spiritually. Plus you still have daily demands and responsibilities. And you also need lots of time for respite and self-care. So I always encourage mourners to "dose" their grief. In other words, I suggest that you actively and intentionally mourn in short spurts followed by appropriate rest and renewal.

3. Explore memories of your attachments
Healing grief always involves going backward before you can go forward. And remembering is the main way in which you go backward.

All attachments and loves are formed in certain places and moments. You will naturally associate your WOLs with these places and moments. In fact, these places and moments are where your WOLs "live." Now, to better understand and integrate your grief, you must work on reviewing and sometimes even digging into those memories.

If you have photos and/or videos documenting your WOLs, that's a good place to start. Spend time looking them over and remembering all the reasons you became attached and what the attachment was like. Gathering up special objects and memorabilia associated with your WOLs can also be a difficult but ultimately healing activity.

Talking to other people about the attachments that gave rise to your WOLs can also be helpful. This is especially true if those you're talking to also have a personal connection to the special people, places, and moments. Expressing yourself can be helpful, but so too is hearing the other people's perspectives. Sometimes learning more about certain attachments can give you new perspectives that help you place your experiences into a larger context.

Finally, visiting the places associated with your WOLs can be a profoundly moving and revealing thing to do. Sometimes in grief we're afraid of embracing old memories because we think they'll be too powerful and hurt too much. But when we do things like return to evocative places, we often realize that the feelings we experience are less powerful than we imagined. Often, exposing ourselves to memories can help make them more approachable.

4. Develop a new self-identity apart from the old attachments
The story of a human life is always a story of change.

Who you were when your attachments and loves formed and grew is not who you are today. Life losses result in you being a changed person.

So part of your grief work after any WOL is exploring how it impacts your self-identity. Who are you now? What do you care about? How do you spend your time and other resources? What do you imagine for your future?

There are many ways to actively work on developing your new sense of self. Talking to other people about your life story and changing roles is one way. Investigating your options is another. When you visit new places, take classes, make vision boards, try new volunteer roles, meet new people, and try new activities, you are working on figuring out who you are now and want to be in the years to come.

This is not to say that you must abandon the old attachments underlying your WOLs. Where love was once it often remains. But those former attachments and loves may now take on new forms. For example, possibly one of your past loves *was* but no longer *is*. Or possibly one of your attachments is still ongoing but now has different features and qualities.

For example, if you're physically separated from someone you care about—say they've moved to a different part of the country or world—your love for them continues, but your relationship with them may necessarily change. You might start spending more time in the physical company of other people while changing the old relationship from one of presence to one of less-frequent virtual presence (texting, video calls, etc.).

Or if you transition from one job to another, you might lose touch with your former coworkers. Your self-identity as part of the old group might potentially evolve into your new self-identity as part of a new group. Or maybe you've arrived at a stage in your life in which you will no longer have colleagues. If so, considering how to fill what might feel like a void may become part of your self-identity grief work.

When it comes to the evolution of your self-identity and changing attachments, you get to decide what feels right for you. You may not have been in control of the transition itself. In fact, you may not have wanted the change to happen in the first place. However, in the aftermath, you do get to choose how you will respond, how you might build new attachments, and how or if the old attachment will live on in your continued life.

Spending your time and attention figuring these things out is an important part of your grief work. You might want to consider seeing a counselor to work on your changing self-identity secondary to your life losses. A compassionate counselor can help affirm your struggles, ask thoughtful questions, and provide ideas for helpful next steps.

5. Search for meaning

As you're sharing the story of your WOLs with people—acknowledging the losses, embracing the pain, and exploring the memories—you will naturally find yourself searching for meaning.

When we're busy living our daily lives, not many of us make time to routinely ponder the meaning of life and death, and whether or not we are pursuing our deepest values and passions. Instead, we're understandably caught up in what has to be done today, tomorrow, and next week. But sometimes things happen that stop us in our tracks—things that makes us examine the circumstances of our lives and consider revised choices or new directions.

Loss is one such event. As discussed, the pain of loss forces us to slow down and turn inward. It is a time in which we naturally pause and consider the big questions of human life. Why are we here? Why did this loss have to happen? What am I going to do with this loss?

For example, if a marriage is ending, it's normal to ponder what the relationship has meant in the story of your life. Why did you marry? What was good about the marriage? What was bad about the marriage? Was that portion of your life well-spent or misspent? What are the life lessons you can take away from the relationship? Will your partner's life continue to intersect with yours, and if so, how? And what does all this mean?

Notice that the search for meaning in grief is not only backward-looking. It's also forward-looking. You are probably wondering what your future will be like under the new circumstances. You may be searching for new attachments to give your life continued meaning. You might be reconsidering your passions and purpose, feeling empty, aimless, or stuck for a period of time.

All aspects of the search for meaning in grief are normal and necessary. I encourage you to take all your inner thoughts and feelings about meaning and purpose and move them to the outside in various ways. Again, talking about these matters to people who care about you can be very helpful. Spiritual practices such as prayer, meditation, journaling, yoga, spending time in nature, and attending services or events are also good outlets to assist you in your search for meaning.

In fact, I consider the search for meaning in grief primarily a spiritual quest. I urge you to consider spending at least a few minutes each day on spiritual self-care of some kind, whatever that looks like for you.

6. Reach out to others for support—now and always
How are you at sharing your innermost thoughts and feelings with other people? You may or may not be someone who has always been open in this way.

If you are, you've likely already been discussing your WOLs with those closest to you. If so, I hope you've found at least one person who is a careful, nonjudgmental listener. On the other hand, if your inner circle hasn't been supportive, you may be well served to seek additional outside support.

However, if you are someone who tends to keep their worries bottled up inside, perhaps you can commit yourself to trying to make a shift in that tendency. Your mourning work requires you to express your grief, because, as I said, the act of expression is what catalyzes the grief to soften over time. And when it comes to telling other people, the act of honest, vulnerable expression also fosters support and strengthens relationships.

Regardless of which group you're in, I encourage you to make time today to tell someone who cares for you about what's weighing on your heart and soul. Send a text, make a phone call, write an email, arrange to have coffee, drop by for a visit. Let this person know you've been learning more about the other losses and have identified at least one WOL you're struggling with. Tell them you'd appreciate their listening ear and support.

You need other people to help you with your WOLs. And they need you to help them with their WOLs as well. We as human beings are social creatures. We are built to live and thrive in relationships and community. Reaching out for mutual support in times of grief and hardship should be the standard practice—not the exception.

Over time, actively, intentionally working on the six needs of mourning is what will allow you to integrate your grief and move forward in life with renewed meaning and purpose. You will know it's time to turn to the six needs of mourning whenever you are experiencing grief symptoms. If you're feeling sad, angry, guilty, fearful, confused, stuck, or ambivalent about a loss, that means you need to give attention to it. Likewise, if you find yourself thinking, worrying, or wondering about a loss, that means you need to openly acknowledge it.

I would remind you that the consequences of not attending to the six needs of mourning can be devastating. Unacknowledged, unmourned loss becomes carried grief, which in turn often results in the potential of chronic depression, anxiety, physical illness, relationship difficulties, addictive behaviors, and more. Because other losses are at risk of being disenfranchised in our culture, they are more likely to result in carried grief.

So if you feel or think it, share it. Do that over and over again until the grief symptoms soften, your WOLs become fully integrated into bittersweet parts of your life story, and you feel fully engaged with your current life, loves, and attachments.

THE IMPORTANCE OF AUTHENTICITY

You may have noticed that I sometimes use the phrase "authentic mourning" to describe the essential process of expressing and healing grief. When I encourage you to authentically mourn, I'm asking you to be completely open and honest.

We sometimes underplay our grief, especially for the other losses. This is because we know these types of losses are often not socially sanctioned. We may feel we're being overly dramatic, needy, or weak if we tell other people how very upset or impacted we really are.

Psychologists sometimes talk about a concept called "congruence." Congruence means that your outer words and behaviors align with your inner feelings and thoughts. The outside matches the inside.

Congruence is essential because it feels right. It's truthful and genuine. Incongruence, on the other hand, feels wrong. It's withholding and dishonest.

When it comes to mourning your other losses, only honesty works. It can take courage to be fully honest about your grief, to be vulnerable enough to show others what's inside you. But here I encourage you to understand the importance of being authentic with your grief and with your mourning.

Your true, raw grief is not shameful. Any shame you might feel about authentically mourning it is often a result of unhealthy cultural taboos and stigmas. So whatever your feelings and thoughts are on the inside, they need authentic representation on the outside. They need you to give them full, accurate, honest voice.

If you are afraid or reticent to mourn fully and authentically, consider starting by writing down your thoughts and feelings. This is a more private, safer method of mourning. Also try talking to your most empathetic, nonjudgmental friend. Tell them one thing you've been afraid to express aloud, then see how they respond. Usually mourners find that any thoughts and feelings they've been holding back for fear of sounding abnormal or foolish are not only understood but frequently shared by others.

There is nothing wrong with you, and there is nothing wrong with your grief. Again, strive to express it authentically. Whatever you are feeling and thinking, mourn it honestly and fully. It's the only way to heal and live and love fully each precious remaining day of your life.

REACHING A NEW NORMAL

Eventually, expressing grief symptoms authentically and fully over time leads to what I call "reconciliation." This is when we have integrated our WOLs into our life stories and are no longer experiencing pronounced grief thoughts and feelings. We've worked our way to a new normal.

Reconciliation is a new equilibrium. It's a plateau where we once again feel stable and content.

In reconciliation, we're different people than we were on the last plateau. We've lost more, and we've learned more. We've grieved again, and we've mourned again. But we're also experiencing a moment in which life feels good again. Through allowing ourselves to mourn, we've come out of the dark and into the light.

Obviously, our new normal is hard-won and often bittersweet. Because life is constant change, and change brings loss, in reconciliation we also realize that more loss will be coming our way. We may experience some anticipatory grief if we know of specific losses that are likely around the corner.

Despite its many losses, life is a privilege. We are here but a short while. And while we're here, we can choose to live on purpose and love deeply every day—even during times of loss and grief.

PART THREE

GRIEF AND MOURNING
AS A WAY OF LIFE

"Life is about not knowing, having to change,
taking the moment and making the best of it, without knowing
what's going to happen next. Delicious ambiguity."

— Gilda Radner

I often reflect that human life is equal parts love and loss.

At times, we like to pretend otherwise. Our culture generally practices mutual pretense when it comes to loss—let's agree to overlook the hard stuff and focus on the good stuff. For some, toxic positivity is alive and well in North America. The pursuit of happiness! Acquiring cool belongings! Seeking pleasure! Having fun with friends and family!

But for every attachment, there's a loss on the horizon. That's because the circumstances of life are in constant flux. Again, anytime we gain something new, we're giving something else up.

No matter how devotedly we love and try to safeguard our attachments, the globe spins. The years pass. And things change.

People get sick.

People age.

People die.

Pets too.

Relationships sputter and end.

People move away.

Normal life transitions unfold.

People betray us.

We betray ourselves.

Passions ebb and flow.

Belongings come and go.

Fortunes rise and fall.

Beliefs shift.

And through it all, we learn and we grow. We are constantly changing, waking up as new people each and every day.

And with every change affecting an attachment or love, there is loss and there is grief.

ACKNOWLEDGING EVERY LOSS

Have you ever noticed that older people seem to adapt to living with loss? By the time they are in their sixties, many people have suffered a variety of life losses. Some would suggest they just grin and bear it.

I propose that grinning and bearing it isn't the best path. Allowing oneself to grieve and mourn is.

My hope is that you would agree that our culture needs to get better at acknowledging loss and supporting people in pain. We like to celebrate joyful occasions and announce good news. We should be just as open about grieving losses and announcing more challenging, often sad news. In fact, we should probably be even more forthcoming about the losses and the grief because that's when we most need the social support.

I encourage all of us to get into the habit of expressing grief whenever we feel it. When any loss that impacts us comes along, we should talk about it. We should also invite the people we care about to share their challenges with us. We should consider that every "catching-up," "how-are-you-doing" conversation with the people we love should be part celebratory, part neutral, and part loss-related.

Talking about loss should not be seen as shameful or burdensome. It is simply an accurate reflection of how life actually is. It is congruent and it is honest. And honesty and empathy always lead to the most authentic, well-lived life.

EVERYTHING BELONGS

We can't control life and death. We can't control other people. We can't control most of the circumstances that create loss in our lives.

We may not like loss, but we have to admit that it happens frequently. It's an unavoidable, uncontrollable part of human life.

All of which is to say that loss belongs.

We should expect it. We should acknowledge it. And we should even learn to befriend it, because loss is the price we pay for love and attachment, which are among the greatest gifts of our human lives. Loss is not the exception; it's the rule.

THE FREEDOM TO MOURN

"Everything can be taken from a man but one thing: the last of the human freedoms—to choose one's attitude in any given set of circumstances, to choose one's own way," wrote Holocaust survivor Viktor Frankl.

When faced with loss of any kind, we get to choose how we will respond. It's natural to grieve—to be shocked, afraid, sad, angry, guilty, ambivalent, etc. But it's also natural to mourn—

to express our grief openly and honestly for as long as it takes, thereby softening our grief and integrating the new loss into the ongoing story of our life.

Remember that you're free to mourn. Each and every day, you're free to be open, honest, and kind to others. Come what may, you're free to express how you think and feel, so long as you're not lashing out at and hurting others.

The next time you talk to a friend, I challenge you to ask them how they're doing. It's probably something you routinely ask. But this time, ask them to share something difficult or challenging as well as the neutral and good things they're likely to offer up.

Then it's your turn to share. Tell them about your WOLs. Tell them what you're working on. If you want to, you can ask if they have any supportive counsel or learned any helpful lessons in dealing with their own life losses.

A FINAL WORD

Life and grief are not mutually exclusive.

Yes, I know that when we're grieving, it can feel like life comes to a halt. As I said earlier, loss tends to stop us in our tracks. In the face of life losses, we do need to slow down and turn inward. We need to acknowledge what happened and take the time to mourn well and integrate them into our lives, our living, and our loving.

But still, life all around us keeps going, and grief is a significant part of life.

I hope this exploration of the other losses has helped you see that loss is normal and that loss, grief, and mourning belong just as much as happiness, joy, and celebration do.

If you picked up this book, it's probably because your WOLs are trying to get your attention right now. You may have some unmourned losses that require your awareness, time, attention, and expression. I hope you will apply yourself to your grief work and find ways to mourn openly and authentically. I hope you will engage with all six of the needs of mourning outlined in this book. Give yourself permission to take as much time as you need for your symptoms to soften and for you to feel like you're reaching a place of reconciliation.

The sooner and more wholeheartedly you begin daily active mourning, the sooner you are likely to integrate your WOLs and have more energy and time to devote to remaining and new attachments in your life.

Still, there are no rewards for speed in grief, so please find the pace and methods that work for you.

Thank you for the privilege of allowing me to explore this important topic with you. I hope you will begin applying what you've learned to meet, befriend, and heal all of your losses along life's path. I hope you will share with friends and family what you've learned as well. I hope you will join me in helping make grief and mourning a normal, accepted, healing way of life.

I hope we meet one day.

YOUR NOTES ON OTHER LOSSES

ABOUT THE AUTHOR

Alan D. Wolfelt, Ph.D., is a respected author and educator on the topics of companioning others and healing in grief. He serves as Director of the Center for Loss and Life Transition and is on the faculty at the University of Colorado Medical

 School's Department of Family Medicine. Dr. Wolfelt has written many bestselling books on healing in grief, including *Understanding Your Grief*, *Healing Your Grieving Heart*, and *Grief One Day at a Time*. Visit www.centerforloss.com to learn more about grief and loss and to order Dr. Wolfelt's books.

The Hope and Healing Series
Concise books of wisdom and comfort

Readers and counselors often ask Dr. Wolfelt to write books on specialized topics not well-covered elsewhere in the grief literature. He created the Hope and Healing Series to fulfill their requests. These short books focus in on particular types of loss and aspects of grief that while distinct, are not uncommon. They affect many millions of people worldwide, each of whom deserves affirmation, support, and guidance for their unique circumstances.

All Dr. Wolfelt's publications can be ordered by mail from:
Companion Press, 3735 Broken Bow Road, Fort Collins, CO 80526
(970) 226-6050 • www.centerforloss.com

First Aid for Broken Hearts

Life is both wonderful and devastating. It graces us with joy, and it breaks our hearts. If your heart is broken, this book is for you.

Loss may be an unavoidable part of human life, but it doesn't have to prevent you from living well. You can and will survive this. Actually, if

you adopt this guide's basic principles, revealed and tested by Dr. Wolfelt, you will even go on to thrive.

ISBN 978-1-61722-281-8
118 pages • softcover • $9.95

All Dr. Wolfelt's publications can be ordered by mail from:
Companion Press, 3735 Broken Bow Road, Fort Collins, CO 80526
(970) 226-6050 • www.centerforloss.com

Understanding Your Grief [SECOND EDITION]

This book is Dr. Wolfelt's most comprehensive, covering the essential lessons that mourners have taught him in his four decades of working

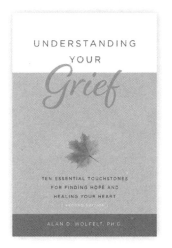

with the bereaved. In compassionate, down-to-earth language, *Understanding Your Grief* describes ten touchstones—or trail markers—that are essential physical, emotional, cognitive, social, and spiritual signs for mourners to look for on their journey through grief.

Think of your grief as a wilderness— a vast, inhospitable forest. You must journey through this wilderness. In the wilderness of your grief, the touchstones are your trail markers. They are the signs that let you know you are on the right path. When you learn to identify and rely on the touchstones, you will find your way to hope and healing.

ISBN 978-1-617223-07-5 • 240 pages • softcover • $14.95

All Dr. Wolfelt's publications can be ordered by mail from:
Companion Press, 3735 Broken Bow Road, Fort Collins, CO 80526
(970) 226-6050 • www.centerforloss.com